WHAT MAKES FIRE BURN?

By Walter LaPlante

Gareth Stevens
PUBLISHING

Please visit our website, www.garethstevens.com. For a free color catalog of all our high-quality books, call toll free 1-800-542-2595 or fax 1-877-542-2596.

Library of Congress Cataloging-in-Publication Data

LaPlante, Walter, author.
 What makes fire burn? / Walter LaPlante.
    pages cm. — (Everyday mysteries)
 Includes bibliographical references and index.
ISBN 978-1-4824-3844-4 (pbk.)
ISBN 978-1-4824-3845-1 (6 pack)
ISBN 978-1-4824-3846-8 (library binding)
1. Fire—Juvenile literature. 2. Combustion—Juvenile literature. I. Title. II. Series:
Everyday mysteries.
 TP265.L37 2016
 541.361—dc23

                         2015026353

Published in 2016 by
Gareth Stevens Publishing
111 East 14th Street, Suite 349
New York, NY 10003

Copyright © 2016 Gareth Stevens Publishing

Designer: Katelyn E. Reynolds
Editor: Kristen Nelson

Photo credits: Cover, p. 1 Africa Studio/Shutterstock.com; pp. 3–24 (background) Natutik/Shutterstock.com; p. 5 Jaktana phongphuek/Shutterstock.com; p. 7 snapgalleria/Shutterstock.com; p. 9 (inset) oorka/Shutterstock.com; p. 9 (main) Andrew Koturanov/Shutterstock.com; p. 11 Stocksnapper/Shutterstock.com; p. 13 viki2win/Shutterstock.com; p. 15 pogonici/Shutterstock.com; p. 17 easyshutter/Shutterstock.com; p. 19 PAKULA PIOTR/Shutterstock.com; p. 21 Colorcocktail/Shutterstock.com.

Printed in the United States of America

CPSIA compliance information: Batch #CW16GS: For further information contact Gareth Stevens, New York, New York at 1-800-542-2595.

CONTENTS

Make a Wish 4

Matter Basics. 6

The Power of Three 8

It's on Fire! 14

Flames 16

Giving Fire 18

Harmful Fire 20

Glossary. 22

For More Information 23

Index 24

Boldface words appear in the glossary.

Make a Wish!

Have you ever watched someone light birthday candles? They might use matches or a lighter. Then, fire seems to come from nowhere! The **process** of creating fire and burning is called combustion. Get ready to learn how it works!

Matter Basics

From bones to flowers, all matter is made up of atoms. Atoms are bonded, or tied, to each other in different ways to form all kinds of matter. Combustion is a **reaction** that causes these bonds to break.

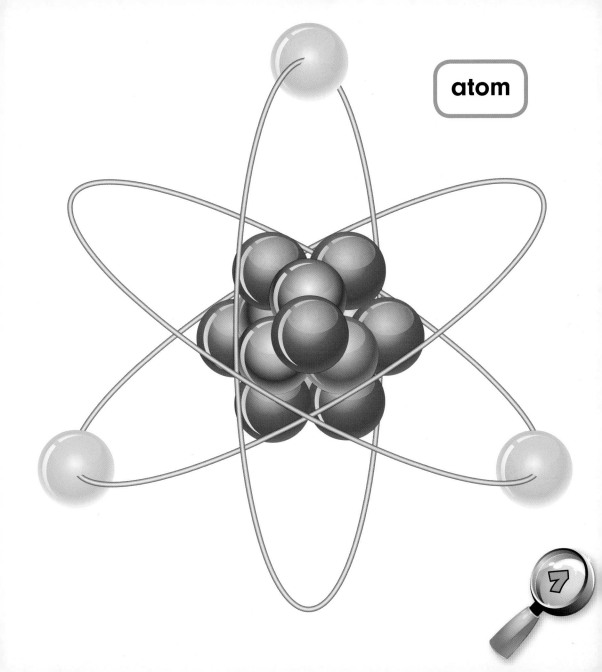

atom

The Power of Three

In order for something to catch fire, three things are needed. One is easy to find because it's in the air around us—oxygen. Oxygen is the gas people must breathe to live. It also helps a fire burn!

oxygen atom

Fire needs heat to happen. Heat can come from the **friction** of a match being struck against a matchbox. It may come from a superhot lightning strike or from the heat created by something that's already burning.

The final piece needed to make fire is fuel. Fuel is what's consumed, or taken in, by burning. Wood or coal are often burned, but fuel for a fire can be anything, including cloth, grass, or rubber. Some fuels need a higher heat than others to burn.

It's on Fire!

Once matter—or fire's fuel—is hot enough, the bonds between its atoms break apart. The atoms then bond to oxygen in the air to make water and gases. It looks like the matter is breaking down. It's burning!

Flames

Have you ever looked closely at the flame on a birthday candle? It's rounded on the bottom and pointed on top. Earth's **gravity** gives it this shape! Flames look blue on the bottom. That's the hottest part!

16

Giving Fire

Combustion is a big part of our lives. A burning fire can keep us warm and give us light. Combustion is even part of how light bulbs work. We need it to make **electricity** at **power plants**, too!

Harmful Fire

Once something catches fire, it can't be unburned. Matter is forever changed by combustion—and it may cause great harm. That's important to keep in mind when you're around fire. Be careful not to burn yourself or things around you!

MAKING FIRE

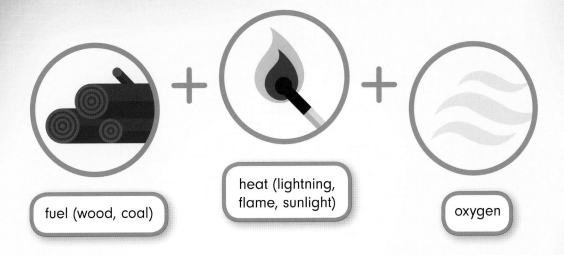

fuel (wood, coal)

heat (lightning, flame, sunlight)

oxygen

=

combustion

GLOSSARY

electricity: the energy, or power, that makes machines and lights work

friction: the force that slows motion between two objects touching each other

gravity: the force that pulls objects toward Earth's center

power plant: a place where the electricity for an area is made

process: the set of steps that move something forward

reaction: the process by which matter is changed

FOR MORE INFORMATION

BOOKS

Brown, Jordan D. *Science Stunts: Fun Feats of Physics.* Watertown, MA: Charlesbridge Publishing, 2016.

Ripley, Catherine. *How? The Most Awesome Question and Answer Book About Nature, Animals, People, Places, and You!* Berkeley, CA: Publishers Group West, 2012.

WEBSITES

Combustion
scienceforkids.kidipede.com/chemistry/reactions/combustion/
Read more about how fire happens, and watch a video to learn exactly what a flame is.

Fire Facts for Kids
sciencekids.co.nz/sciencefacts/fire.html
How hot is that candle's flame? Find out that—and more—on this site.

INDEX

atoms 6, 14

bond 6, 14

burn 4, 8, 10, 12, 14, 18, 20

combustion 4, 6, 18, 20, 21

flame 16

fuel 12, 14, 21

heat 10, 12, 21

lighter 4

lightning 10

matches 4, 10

oxygen 8, 14, 21